Copyright © Curiosities Bound 2021
All rights reserved.

ISBN: 9798744970314
Published 2021 on KDP

The content contained within this book may not be reproduced, duplicated, or transmitted without direct written permission from the author or the publisher.

Created by Audra L. Jones
Curiosities Bound
www.CuriositiesBound.com

Contents

Using Your Gardening Journal - 3

Watering Tips - 5

The Spring Garden - 7

- 9   Seed & Plant Logs
- 17   Weekly Tasks
- 31   Shopping Lists
- 35   Garden Projects
- 39   Garden Notes

The Summer Garden - 47

- 49   Seed & Plant Logs
- 51   Weekly Tasks
- 71   Shopping Lists
- 75   Garden Projects
- 79   Garden Notes

The Fall Garden - 87

- 89   Seed & Plant Logs
- 97   Weekly Tasks
- 111   Shopping Lists
- 115   Garden Projects
- 119   Garden Notes

The Winter Garden - 127

- 129   Seed & Plant Logs
- 137   Weekly Tasks
- 151   Shopping Lists
- 155   Garden Projects
- 159   Garden Notes

Garden Layouts - 167

Works Cited - 183

Using Your Gardening Journal

- This journal is divided into the four seasons- Spring, Summer, Fall and Winter. After each season's tips page, there are logs for seed starting and planting, weekly tasks, projects, and shopping lists. Don't see what you want to record? Add these activities to the notes pages or anywhere there are lines.
- The grid pages at the end of the journal are perfect for sketching your beds. Number, letter or label each to help locate vareities later. Color pencil or highlighter pen is good for adding dimension and interest.
- You can even cut up your seed packets and tape into the framed or grid areas. They make good reminders, and some seed packets are beautiful little works of art.
- And don't forget to note your garden's visitors- birds, butterflies, chipmunks to name a few. Take pictures and add to the framed back pages or sketch when time allows. Make your journal yours, interesting and useful!

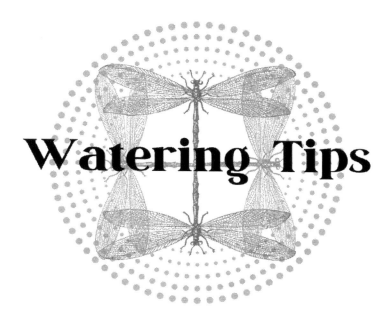

Watering Tips

- It's the roots that need water, not the leaves. Wetting the flowers and leaves can harm plants and wastes water. Reference seed packets for flowers and vegetables.
- Water only when needed. Watch the weather, and reduce watering frequency after a heavy rainfall. Too much water can be just as damaging to plants as too little. Think about automatic timers if forgetting to water is a concern.
- Water thoroughly. Perennials, shrubs and trees concentrate their roots in the top 12", and water may take hours to get down 6-12" in heavy soil, whereas grass and annual roots are in the top 6".
- Water early. Watering in the morning gives leaves time to dry out if you did get them wet. Dry foliage is healthiest and plant diseases are less likely to start.
- Mulch, mulch, mulch. Mulch all your beds to reduce runoff and to slow evaporation.
- Use the right tools. Soaker hoses and irrigation systems are best for evenly watering roots.

The Spring Garden

- Spring is the perfect time to inspect your garden and plan accordingly.
- Look for and make note of damaged plants, beds that need to be cleaned out, and hardscaping that needs attention or repair.
- Plan for new features in your garden- new beds, walls, water elements.
- Spring is also a good time to clean garden features- bird baths, feeders, fountains.
- Testing and fertilizing soil may also be done now. Check online for best testing practices in your area.
- Pruning shrubs that are damaged or dead can be done in spring, as well as, flowering shrubs that bloom from new wood (this year's growth).
- Do not cut stems that bloom from old wood. Search for your plant online if you are not sure which can be cut now.
- Dividing and transplanting perennials that bloom in the summer and fall can be done in spring- opposite season of when they bloom is an easy way to remember so as not to disrupt their bloom cycle.
- Putting out any necessary supports (think peonies and clematis) is ideal now- clean and paint beforehand.
- And finally, watch out for that late last frost. Monitor and cover as needed. Now you're ready for the perfect summer garden!

Seed & Plant Log

Seed or Plant	Variety	Weeks Before Last Frost	Date Planted	Days to Germinate
Notes				
Notes				
Notes				
Notes				
Notes				
Notes				
Notes				

Seed & Plant Log

Seed or Plant	Variety	Weeks Before Last Frost	Date Planted	Days to Germinate
Notes				
Notes				
Notes				
Notes				
Notes				
Notes				
Notes				

Seed & Plant Log

Seed or Plant	Variety	Weeks Before Last Frost	Date Planted	Days to Germinate
Notes				
Notes				
Notes				
Notes				
Notes				
Notes				
Notes				

Seed & Plant Log

Seed or Plant	Variety	Weeks Before Last Frost	Date Planted	Days to Germinate
Notes				
Notes				
Notes				
Notes				
Notes				
Notes				
Notes				

Weekly Tasks

Plant/Variety	Transplant/Divide	Trim	Fertilize	Date	Notes

Weekly Tasks

Plant/Variety	Transplant/Divide	Trim	Fertilize	Date	Notes

Weekly Tasks

Plant/Variety	Transplant/Divide	Trim	Fertilize	Date	Notes

Weekly Tasks

Plant/Variety	Transplant/Divide	Trim	Fertilize	Date	Notes

Weekly Tasks

Plant/Variety	Transplant/Divide	Trim	Fertilize	Date	Notes

Weekly Tasks

Plant/Variety	Transplant/Divide	Trim	Fertilize	Date	Notes

Weekly Tasks

Plant/Variety	Transplant/Divide	Trim	Fertilize	Date	Notes

Weekly Tasks

Plant/Variety	Transplant/Divide	Trim	Fertilize	Date	Notes

Weekly Tasks

Plant/Variety	Transplant/Divide	Trim	Fertilize	Date	Notes

Weekly Tasks

Plant/Variety	Transplant/Divide	Trim	Fertilize	Date	Notes

Weekly Tasks

Plant/Variety	Transplant/Divide	Trim	Fertilize	Date	Notes

Weekly Tasks

Plant/Variety	Transplant/Divide	Trim	Fertilize	Date	Notes

Weekly Tasks

Plant/Variety	Transplant/Divide	Trim	Fertilize	Date	Notes

Shopping List

DATE

Shopping List

DATE

Garden Projects

DATE

Garden Projects

DATE

Garden Notes

Garden Notes

Garden Notes

Garden Notes

The Summer Garden

- Tidy up! Trim back any foliage that has turned brown and cut off any spent flowers on perennials.
- Prune any spring flowering shrubs that have finished blooming on old wood (last year's growth)- lilacs, forsysthias and viburnums. Check online if unsure what growth your shrub produces.
- Trim and shape evergreen boxwoods and holly shrubs. Electric trimmers are perfect for this.
- Pull those weeds! This neverending task is a little easier if beds are mulched and you pull when weeds are small.
- Add annuals if you have any empty spots or need to add some color.
- Fertilize once a week or every third time you water. Some flowers need more than others so reference online sites or seed packets.
- Keep that birdbath clean and full of fresh water. Your birds will thank you by returning and putting on a show.
- Enjoy your spring and summer labors by displaying those beautiful flowers and sharing various veggies.

Seed & Plant Log

Seed or Plant	Variety	Weeks Before Last Frost	Date Planted	Days to Germinate
Notes				
Notes				
Notes				
Notes				
Notes				
Notes				
Notes				

Seed & Plant Log

Seed or Plant	Variety	Weeks Before Last Frost	Date Planted	Days to Germinate
Notes				
Notes				
Notes				
Notes				
Notes				
Notes				
Notes				

Seed & Plant Log

Seed or Plant	Variety	Weeks Before Last Frost	Date Planted	Days to Germinate
Notes				
Notes				
Notes				
Notes				
Notes				
Notes				
Notes				

Seed & Plant Log

Seed or Plant	Variety	Weeks Before Last Frost	Date Planted	Days to Germinate
Notes				
Notes				
Notes				
Notes				
Notes				
Notes				
Notes				

Weekly Tasks

Plant/Variety	Transplant/Divide	Trim	Fertilize	Date	Notes

Weekly Tasks

Plant/Variety	Transplant/Divide	Trim	Fertilize	Date	Notes

Weekly Tasks

Plant/Variety	Transplant/Divide	Trim	Fertilize	Date	Notes

Weekly Tasks

Plant/Variety	Transplant/Divide	Trim	Fertilize	Date	Notes

Weekly Tasks

Plant/Variety	Transplant/Divide	Trim	Fertilize	Date	Notes

Weekly Tasks

Plant/Variety	Transplant/Divide	Trim	Fertilize	Date	Notes

Weekly Tasks

Plant/Variety	Transplant/Divide	Trim	Fertilize	Date	Notes

Weekly Tasks

Plant/Variety	Transplant/Divide	Trim	Fertilize	Date	Notes

Weekly Tasks

Plant/Variety	Transplant/Divide	Trim	Fertilize	Date	Notes

Weekly Tasks

Plant/Variety	Transplant/Divide	Trim	Fertilize	Date	Notes

Weekly Tasks

Plant/Variety	Transplant/Divide	Trim	Fertilize	Date	Notes

Weekly Tasks

Plant/Variety	Transplant/Divide	Trim	Fertilize	Date	Notes

Weekly Tasks

Plant/Variety	Transplant/Divide	Trim	Fertilize	Date	Notes

Shopping List

DATE

DATE

Garden Projects

DATE

Garden Projects

DATE

Garden Notes

Garden Notes

Garden Notes

Garden Notes

The Fall Garden

- Collect dried seed from veggies and open-pollinated flowers. Save and sow next year in another part of your garden.
- Gather flowers and herbs for drying. Be sure to leave some for the birds!
- Cut back hydrangea and yarrow and enjoy indoors.
- Take cuttings now. Small plants will be easier to transplant in the spring.
- Clean bird feeders and tools before storing.
- Winterize any water features that won't be utilized in the cold.
- Enrich beds with manure or compost with an even layer over the soil.
- Cut back most perennials, and remember to never place diseased foliage in the compost.
- Continue to water trees and shrubs until the ground freezes or if located in mild or dry winters.

Seed & Plant Log

Seed or Plant	Variety	Weeks Before Last Frost	Date Planted	Days to Germinate
Notes				
Notes				
Notes				
Notes				
Notes				
Notes				
Notes				

Seed & Plant Log

Seed or Plant	Variety	Weeks Before Last Frost	Date Planted	Days to Germinate
Notes				
Notes				
Notes				
Notes				
Notes				
Notes				
Notes				

Seed & Plant Log

Seed or Plant	Variety	Weeks Before Last Frost	Date Planted	Days to Germinate
Notes				
Notes				
Notes				
Notes				
Notes				
Notes				
Notes				

Seed & Plant Log

Seed or Plant	Variety	Weeks Before Last Frost	Date Planted	Days to Germinate
Notes				
Notes				
Notes				
Notes				
Notes				
Notes				
Notes				

Weekly Tasks

Plant/Variety	Transplant/Divide	Trim	Fertilize	Date	Notes

Weekly Tasks

Plant/Variety	Transplant/Divide	Trim	Fertilize	Date	Notes

Weekly Tasks

Plant/Variety	Transplant/Divide	Trim	Fertilize	Date	Notes

Weekly Tasks

Plant/Variety	Transplant/Divide	Trim	Fertilize	Date	Notes

Weekly Tasks

Plant/Variety	Transplant/Divide	Trim	Fertilize	Date	Notes

Weekly Tasks

Plant/Variety	Transplant/Divide	Trim	Fertilize	Date	Notes

Weekly Tasks

Plant/Variety	Transplant/Divide	Trim	Fertilize	Date	Notes

Weekly Tasks

Plant/Variety	Transplant/Divide	Trim	Fertilize	Date	Notes

Weekly Tasks

Plant/Variety	Transplant/Divide	Trim	Fertilize	Date	Notes

Weekly Tasks

Plant/Variety	Transplant/Divide	Trim	Fertilize	Date	Notes

Weekly Tasks

Plant/Variety	Transplant/Divide	Trim	Fertilize	Date	Notes

Weekly Tasks

Plant/Variety	Transplant/Divide	Trim	Fertilize	Date	Notes

Weekly Tasks

Plant/Variety	Transplant/Divide	Trim	Fertilize	Date	Notes

DATE

Shopping List

DATE

Garden Projects

DATE

Garden Projects

DATE

Garden Notes

Garden Notes

Garden Notes

Garden Notes

The Winter Garden

- Take inventory and get organized! This is easier to do in the winter when your gardening tasks are lighter. Do now and your spring will be that much easier.
- Clean tools before storing.
- Start or expand your composting.
- Freshen up old beds, tear down and build new beds or add to existing ones, if you have enough space.
- Organize your seeds and order more, and begin to plan for next year's crop.
- Check stored bulbs once a month for mold and extra moisture.
- Mulching and covering can keep plants alive if freezing temperatures are consistant in your area.
- Add a fun new element to your garden every year. Everyone in the family will look forward to planning and enjoying each year.
- And finally, catch up on your garden journaling and sketching, if needed. Reminice and appreciate your bountiful garden and make way for a fabulous spring!

Seed & Plant Log

Seed or Plant	Variety	Weeks Before Last Frost	Date Planted	Days to Germinate
Notes				
Notes				
Notes				
Notes				
Notes				
Notes				
Notes				

Seed & Plant Log

Seed or Plant	Variety	Weeks Before Last Frost	Date Planted	Days to Germinate
Notes				
Notes				
Notes				
Notes				
Notes				
Notes				
Notes				

Seed & Plant Log

Seed or Plant	Variety	Weeks Before Last Frost	Date Planted	Days to Germinate
Notes				
Notes				
Notes				
Notes				
Notes				
Notes				
Notes				

Seed & Plant Log

Seed or Plant	Variety	Weeks Before Last Frost	Date Planted	Days to Germinate
Notes				
Notes				
Notes				
Notes				
Notes				
Notes				
Notes				

Weekly Tasks

Plant/Variety	Transplant/Divide	Trim	Fertilize	Date	Notes

Weekly Tasks

Plant/Variety	Transplant/Divide	Trim	Fertilize	Date	Notes

Weekly Tasks

Plant/Variety	Transplant/Divide	Trim	Fertilize	Date	Notes

Weekly Tasks

Plant/Variety	Transplant/Divide	Trim	Fertilize	Date	Notes

Weekly Tasks

Plant/Variety	Transplant/Divide	Trim	Fertilize	Date	Notes

Weekly Tasks

Plant/Variety	Transplant/Divide	Trim	Fertilize	Date	Notes

Weekly Tasks

Plant/Variety	Transplant/Divide	Trim	Fertilize	Date	Notes

Weekly Tasks

Plant/Variety	Transplant/Divide	Trim	Fertilize	Date	Notes

Weekly Tasks

Plant/Variety	Transplant/Divide	Trim	Fertilize	Date	Notes

Weekly Tasks

Plant/Variety	Transplant/Divide	Trim	Fertilize	Date	Notes

Weekly Tasks

Plant/Variety	Transplant/Divide	Trim	Fertilize	Date	Notes

Weekly Tasks

Plant/Variety	Transplant/Divide	Trim	Fertilize	Date	Notes

Weekly Tasks

Plant/Variety	Transplant/Divide	Trim	Fertilize	Date	Notes

DATE

Shopping List

DATE

Garden Projects

DATE

Garden Projects

DATE

Garden Notes

Garden Notes

Garden Notes

Garden Notes

My Garden Layout

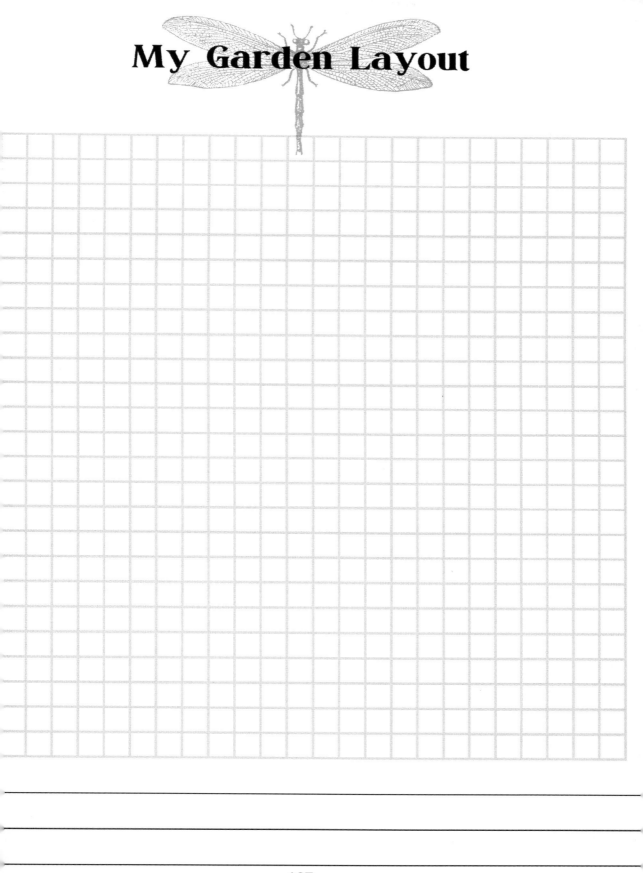

My Garden Layout

My Garden Layout

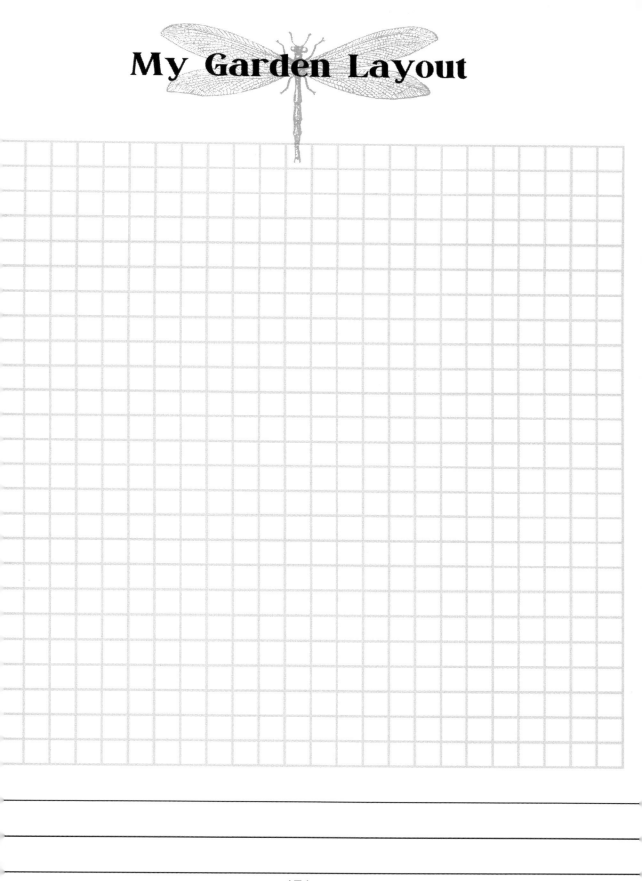

My Garden Layout

My Garden Layout

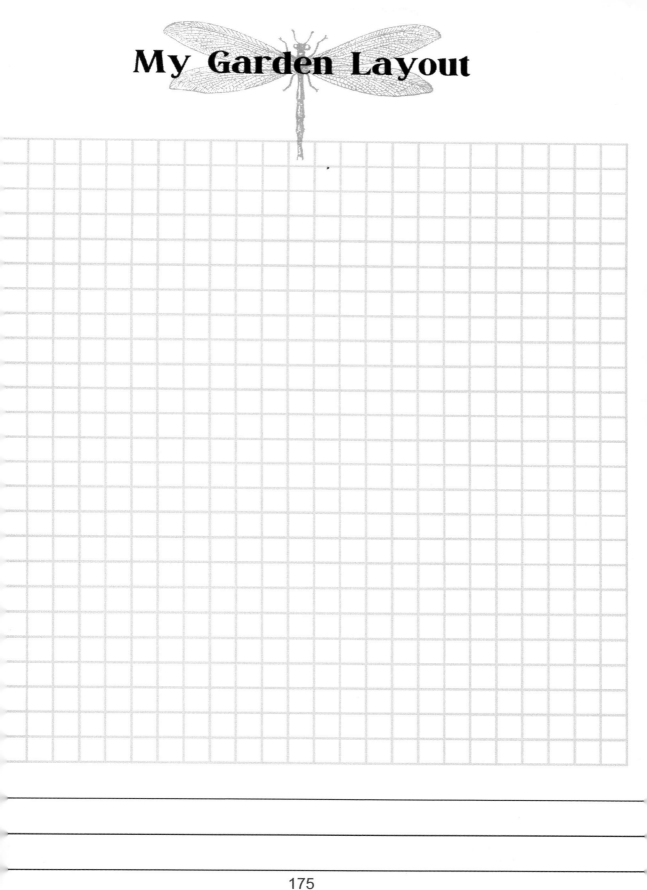

My Garden Layout

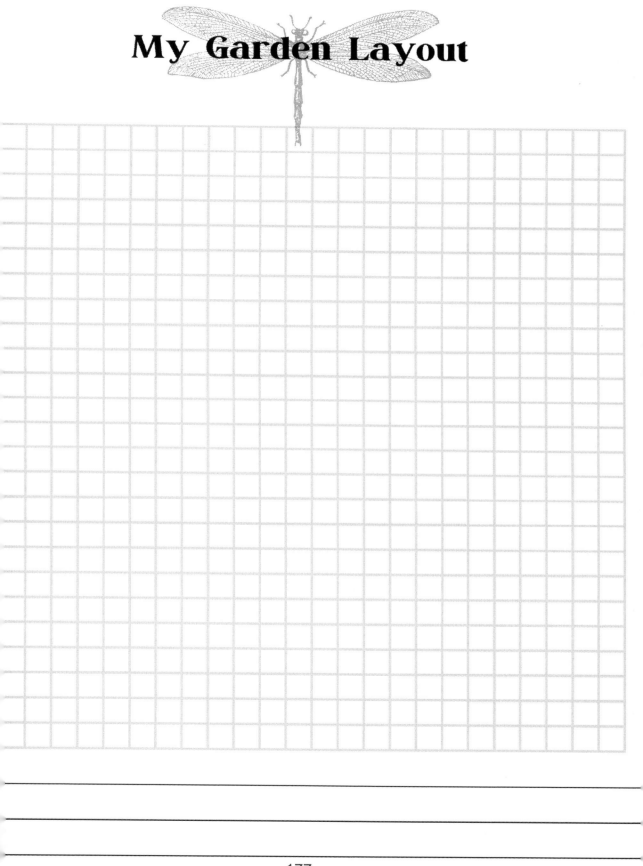

My Garden Layout

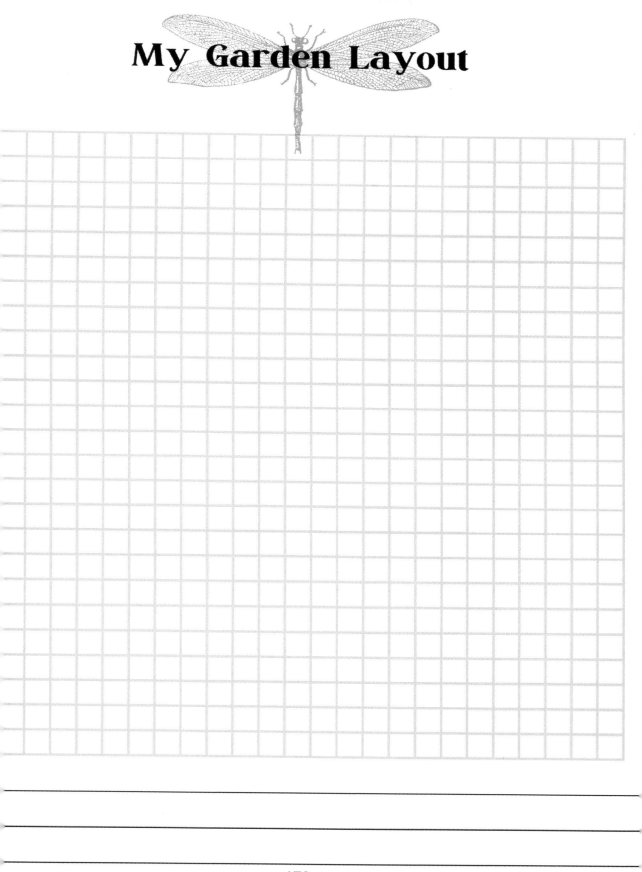

My Garden Layout

Works Cited

Gibson, M. (n.d.). 12 Winter Gardening Tasks. Gardening Channel. Retrieved April 23, 2021, from https://www.gardeningchannel.com/12-winter-gardening-tasks/

Iannotti, M. (2020, October 11). Fall Garden Tasks for a Better Spring Garden. The Spruce. Retrieved April 23, 2021, from https://www.thespruce.com/fall-garden-tasks-for-better-spring-garden-1402441

Kelly, J. (n.d.). How to Plant a Garden in Order of Rows. SFGate. Retrieved April 23, 2021, from https://homeguides.sfgate.com/plant-garden-order-rows-39568.html

LaLiberte, K. (2021, January 25). Watering Tips, When to Water. Gardener's Supply. Retrieved April 25, 2021, from https://www.gardeners.com/how-to/when-to-water/8108.html

Martin, S. (n.d.). 10 Essential Spring Gardening Tasks. Proven Winners. Retrieved April 23, 2021, from https://www.provenwinners.com/learn/early-spring/10-essential-spring-gardening-tasks

Martin, S. (2019, July 22). Seven Essential Summer Gardening Tasks. Garden Crossings. Retrieved April 23, 2021, from https://www.gardencrossings.com/blog/seven-essential-summer-gardening-tasks/

Printed in Great Britain
by Amazon